Presented to:

Never Forget The Difference You've Made

Made in the USA
Las Vegas, NV
14 December 2022

62665364R00066